THE EXTREMITIES

THE
EXTREMITIES
TIMOTHY
KELLY

Oberlin College Press
Oberlin, Ohio

Thanks to the following journals in which these poems appeared, some in earlier forms: *Ars Medica*: "Asymmetry"; *Burnside Review*: "Why It Takes Longer to Make Love When You're 50"; *Crab Creek Review*: "Unbecoming"; *FIELD*: "Diagnosis of Noisy Knees"; *Image*: "Body as Temple" and "Fast"; *JUB*: "Body Optional" and "Three Falls"; *Northwest Review*: "Comealong"; *Pontoon*: "Exposition"; and *Willow Springs*: "Broken Spoke." The poems "On Anatomy Being Destiny" and "Exposition" appeared in the chapbook *Toccata & Fugue* (Floating Bridge Press, 2005).

Special thanks to Lucia Perillo, Susan Christian, Patrick Casey, and Cynthia Pratt, early and invaluable readers of *The Extremities*.

The FIELD Poetry Series, vol. 21
Oberlin College Press, 50 N. Professor Street, Oberlin, OH 44074

www.oberlin.edu/ocpress

Cover photograph © Arno Rafael Minkkinen: *Self-portrait. Fosters Pond, 1989.*
Courtesy Tibor de Nagy Gallery, New York.
Cover and book design: Steve Farkas

Library of Congress Cataloging-in-Publication Data

Kelly, Timothy, 1951-
   The extremities / Timothy Kelly.
      p. cm. — (The Field poetry series ; v. 21)
   ISBN-13: 978-0-932440-33-4 (pbk. : alk. paper)
   ISBN-10: 0-932440-33-9 (pbk. : alk. paper)
   I. Title
   PS3561.E39719E98 2008
   811'.54—dc22
                              2008006304

Contents

1.

On Anatomy Being Destiny

We disarticulate our ankle
with a hundred circumferential cuts,
the crosslaced ligaments isolated,
identified, incised; the snug, bony
mortise and tenon, with effort, prized

apart. Then I have the foot
in my hand, the gray, rubbery,
horn-nailed thing it will take us two
more weeks to unwind, wandering
down through the springtight rigging,
sleek tendon sheaths, the brilliant,
helical twist-lock puzzle

of its bones. First, though, I walk
the foot to the old lab's window
where the day's woolen sky has peached,
and make it jig on the sill, a little
heel-toe my wife taught me
in a bar in Cincinnati in 1979. I
didn't much like her then. Or

the dive with its funky jars
of pinkish pigs' feet lined up
at the registers. But she had danced
there to various fiddling for years
on Fridays, in pleated skirt and
stocking feet, and would again that night,
pivoting crisply, passed laughing
hand to hand. I wouldn't dance. So
she asked me to hold her shoe.

Asymmetry

The ribs, in their flare from the sternum,
are planed back like limbs on a windward bluff,
the long bone combs forced round in a clamshell
ellipse until the ends, aligned and opposed,
are sutured down tight into the long dashed seam
of the spine. Above them, the stem of the neck,
blown bulb of the skull; below, the pedestal

of the pelvis, alabaster birdbath balanced
on telescoped, pikelike legs. There should be
two shoulders; ball, socket and 3-cornered blade
swiveling snug against the ribs, enabling the hand,
in all its mischief and grace, to travel out across

disorder, and grasp. She first showed me, in 1979,
her feet; and when I seized them she bridled
and wouldn't allow me, for months, to examine
them again. They were, it turned out, different;
slightly asymmetrical: the right's toes clawed
and callused, a shoe-size bigger than the left.
It was, in her mind, a deformation, a defining

characteristic, a central, dead-serious defect.
I seized the monster, kissed it; kissed the ankle,
the knee. I begged her let me continue, a Jesuit,
upstream, baptizing and bringing to light all other
stigmatized, sequestered asymmetry.

Body as Temple

1.

Tie the slumped stroke patient
upright in his chair and wheel him
to the tabernacle; nod with him
to the handclaps and whoops
as the sweaty psalms to the body
are sung. The maiden's slim foot
bewitches the king; the king's
sword hums in its scabbard. She
loves him, she loves him not;
the issue is already long-settled,
etched ages ago into the calculus
of our 200 birch-bark bones.

Lord, is it all not beautiful?
Does the beetle not powder
the downed cedar log and
skunk-cabbage uptwist its lanterns
deep in the spring-soaked bog?
Are You not replete in mosquito
as You are in trembling vireo, or
palomino, the stallion we passed
trekking out of the Wallowas,
who cantered to the corner of
his pasture to meet us, shook his white,
tinseled mane over the fence, and,
when I reached up spellbound
to rub his velvet nose, bit my hand?

2.

The body you saw this morning
shucked off like a spring coat
while your lidded eyes swiveled
and your feet pattered and jerked;
the rose body you step daily out of
the shower in, the encumbrance,
albatross, cabinet, short-stay unit,
with legs like Paul Bunyan, trunk
like the ox, and hair springing ruthless
out of every etched crevice. Here

is a picture of you naked at Jemez Springs,
1996, clothes folded neatly on a boulder
at the pool's lip, your raised hand only half-
blocking the camera. Behind you is
the old hippie who droned on about
the minerals we hadn't yet realized our
bodies craved. He took daily infusions
and could now crack nuts with his teeth.
When, at the Last Judgment, the soul

is reunited with the body, it won't be
these creaky, high-mileage models we slip
back into, no. It will, Augustine argued,
be a body uncorrupted, perfected, all
of your lifelong grievances redressed.
And we will shuffle like supermodels
toward the throne, staring at our radiant
hands, listening to the terrible sorting,
the sudden crying out, the impeccable
pronunciation of each arrowed name.

The Eroticised World

1. We passed, on the wetlands boardwalk,
   through stands of cattail higher than our heads,
   clacking and nodding, dry as October corn.
   And the flitting and whistles within them were
   redwings, no question, though we saw, in
   the end, only two: slanted crimson shoulder
   blaze, the *conk-a ree* and trailing buzzy trill.

   And I, still raw then from the ferocious
   novelty of our lovemaking, couldn't see the reed
   sway, or the taut blackberries, or the heron's
   neck coiled to stab, without reaching for you,
   hand feeling back as the chattering kingfisher
   spiraled down like a dropped package, plunged
   in, exploded out, the plucked herring, dime-
   silver, half-swallowed, clamped in his beak.

2. Mornings I'd study the curve of your arm
   because I was dissecting an arm, the long
   forearm muscles tapering to ribbony tendon,
   each gathered at the wrist's cinch like stems
   through the neck of a vase. I was coming to

   understand how fingers worked: the balanced
   mechanics, tensioned lines, tracked pulleys,
   and action fine and subtle enough to cover
   a lover's touch, sliver's end, concise Chopin
   etudes. Now, at work, I take a damaged hand

   in mine and move it slowly, repeatedly,
   through patterns it can no longer do itself. And
   the patient will watch the odd choreography
   sourly, as if not wishing to be reminded of that
   language, that flown ease and fluency, of what
   his larking touch once, unencumbered, could do.

Transport

1. Confirmed by the nuns in our biblical writ
   of dominion, we pithed our frog, incised
   the leg, and peeled the freckled translucence,
   whole cloth, back. And though we had prepared
   ourselves with line drawings and texts:
   the sheathed muscles, slate-blue vessels,
   the glistening whiteness of the joints, we were
   still taken aback by the odd vividness
   of a pulsing, shuddering, still-living thing.

   What God made this creature? the tapering,
   tightly gathered thigh muscle, snapping
   the knee straight in its extractive reflex leap
   away; or made us who could, simultaneously
   sickened and thrilled, take that creature,
   by textbook stages, apart, wiggling out
   in the end the straight pins we'd driven
   earlier, so carefully through its wrists?

2. And how that Friday she kissed me, zero
   warning, my lab partner, by the black brick
   incinerator behind the school, and left me speechless
   and spinning there, ears burning inside my hat,

   prayers answered, world remade. And how she
   ignored me then completely, who didn't call,
   who feared her bullnecked brothers, who pined
   for some word, nod or acknowledgment that

   the unsayable had actually passed between us.
   I went to the St Patrick's Day Show to see her
   sing, and to the party after, where the women,
   paired, step-danced together, trading men's parts,

   mothers showing girls the complex patterns,
   spinning them like tops, then linking arms
   and turning like toothed gears in some seamless,
   foreign, beautifully-machined transmission.

Heaven

More and more I believe
that warmth will be critical,
and nearby, past the *chaises-longues*,
a plunge. I remember the day

F. X. O'Reilly, SJ, delved
into heaven, March, 6th period,
the near westside of Cleveland
in a jacket of clear, hard ice.

Due to the Judgment Day's
Resurrection of the Body,
heaven would have to be
a vast and accommodating

physical space. All those
milling bodies, from Adam
and Abraham onward. Earth
would likely be, he reasoned,

too small. He scratched his chin.
Somewhere bigger, he figured.
Maybe Jupiter.

Every Step Is a Fall Interrupted

1.
Just as the left foot lifts from the ground,
the right swings forward and strikes, and
the left arm above, reciprocating in cadence,
the counter-rotation which neatly conserves
our advancing, insinuating centers. And we
vault over the landed leg as a tree leans
when the sawcut's near through, trunk tipped,
head forward, set to pitch twisting to earth
were it not for the timely, rescuing, still-

oddly-astonishing *next step*. All the pieces
came together for me the week I followed you
up Icicle Creek and into the Enchantments,
your ankle unlocked for each footfall, then
stiffening, with the leg's spin, to translate
the riveting thrust of your hip and leg into
a sequence of fluid, predicate steps. We pitched
camp and zipped together for the first time there,
amid the tarns and stars and gone-gold larches,

and you told me, dipping dreamily in and out
of sleep, about certain orgasms which advance
like Northern Ohio thunderstorms, isolated
on the horizon a long ways off, and fetched
unhurriedly, with stalls, staggers, and a sweet,
saturated certainty, toward the desired end
the core of you rises to, the decisive shift
when you, accelerating to thruway speed,
rhythmically signaling, merge.

2.

Our church, it turned out, was in
the mountains, the scoured rock,
the sky brought down, the shuffling,
imperturbable porcupine. And after
years of tithing, we're suddenly faced
with the seditious grind of bone
on bone, and kneel around the flaming
altar of the campstove, massaging
joints and waiting for some tea with
which to swallow our ibuprofens.

Our children, knuckleheads, hate it:
the bad food, the insects, the wind-
trilled tent. But it speaks to us still
(though we do incline increasingly
to deafness), climbing carefully,
less far, but pressing determinedly,
boot-over-boot, toward sky, source
of warmth, water, and, beyond that,
come sunset, the deep, welded seam of
the Milky Way. Every word breathed
there stands swirling a second, a plume
jetted from the head, a line of dialog
inked in a balloon, floated off tatters
before it can be read.

Overwintering Birds

They quilt the inlet
like marching bands
on windowpane, patterns
dissolving, lines merging,
outliers skimming back
to the correct count and
stagger. The divers tip

and disappear for
improbable spans, bob
up brighteyed half
a world away. Hours
pass with occasional
honks and light orchestral
tuning. Rain drifts. Then,
unprovoked, a passel
of goldeneyes will
explode up, crying,
wingtips smacking water,

and the whole inlet
erupt in a wave of
squalls and squawks,
then settle, with preening
and indignation, as
the reading room of
a great library might
after a shouted string
of epithets from some
smudged stranger, who
stares about wildeyed
in a boxer's crouch,
smothering scolds,
preempting challenge.

Deer Tracks in the Mudflats, Sunrise, Henderson Inlet, April

A midnight high and a minus,
moon-leavened low leaves the basin
drained at five, and the oyster cribs,
salt-rimed, lie supine, like a ward
of sleepers who've thrown off
their sheets in an agitated, febrile
thrash. Herons dot the shallows,
staring down like the gallery
in a surgical theater, and a confusion
of cloven prints, fresh, resolves
quickly, just below the tide-line,
into two parallel lines, doe and fawn
moving, unhurriedly, earlier this
morning, north. Hungry; maybe
lost; maybe looking for a place to cross.
Or maybe they came, as we have,
to spy the great gaggle of transiting,
granite-gray geese, bills tucked,
bobbing, bumping, bussed slowly
north with the sliding tide. Or
to scc thc starry cast gradually yield
to the penciled-in pinks of the day.
Or maybe they came to hear more
clearly the oddly modern music
of the ebb, the tuned tympanis and
pizzicato plinks of water drawn
elastic, in its sinuous, mud-etched
channels, away.

Fast

After two days without food, the edges
of things sharpened, a trick I guessed
my eyes were playing, dividing the edible
ever more starkly from the in-. A rabbit,
hightailing, zigzagged broomstand to
blackberry, and something already tight

in me coiled tighter. And further, when
the long-lashed Appaloosa snuffed me
up and down at the fence, nosing through
my coat for an apple, I stood there empty-
handed, flap-armed, too weak to even say
or sing thanks. Happily, the swallows had
gathered for dusk to do it, their twittering

crosstalk swollen to a cacophonous din
as they dropped one by one from the high
wires to shear openmouthed, cheered, over
the dry, towheaded, windworked field.

Gray's Anatomy

He had the liver, raw purple slab, on wax paper
in a cooler, and had offered neighbors slices as tonic
for iron-poor blood. But by the time I got there,
the carcass hung gutted, headless and skinned,
by a rearfoot tendon from garage rafters. It looked
like a greyhound mid-stride, or a cliff-diver
stopped stiffarmed, ivory-ribbed, a foot above
the water. Raymond, his son, claimed the old
fucker liked the jerky and sausage, but not the actual
killing, and the assembled neighbor boys squinted
down like pirates, nodded sagely and spat.

What I remember was the bunched muscle
around the shoulders; the half-arms, the arcade
of tapering ribs. I thought of *Gray's Anatomy*,
which I had removed months ago to my room,
the man on the cover vertically scored, his right
side peeled like a potato, the warp of muscle in his
upraised arm twisting down like a small, stopped
rapids. I thought of the buck in Pennsylvania,
beginning this day with birdsong and a stream,
and slid, neck twisted, hours later, from the hood
of a chrome-lipped Chrysler in Cleveland,
his mahogany eye dulled, teeth sumac yellow,
and horns like heretical ideas extruded, awaiting
their Jesuit, their arbiter, their quick, decisive,
skull-hatcheting judge.

Animal Locomotion, 1887
University of Pennsylvania

The thoroughbreds, the farm animals
Muybridge had photographed a year
earlier, in California; the prolific nudes,
strolling, churning, performing chores
and the Englishman's scripted tableaux,
were both paid and volunteer, but each
a prim, pale Philadelphian. So where

did his bevy of unreconstructed Quakers
find the nerve to step out of their skirts,
slips, corsets, drawers, and into bleaching
spring sun, to wait on their marks and his
signal, to move uninhibited, incandescent
in front of the gridlike black backdrop,
the clustered shutters tripping off like
a drumroll? They must've wondered

about the old devil, acquitted ten years ago,
despite a candid courtroom confession,
of murdering his wife's lover, point-
blank, with a revolver. Now his mania
was to provide unimpeachable evidence
of how much actually happened in
the space of a single second. Muybridge

could explode a single stride, in cogwheel
increments, across a page, memorialize
your most secret self stepping starkly,
ribs and breasts unbound, down a stage-
rigged set of stairs, flesh answering gravity

frankly, without artifice or romance, and
fixed in finegrained black and white;
every muscle visible, origin, insertion,
firing in logical, flickering, precisely timed
sequences there, just beneath the skin.

Received Wisdom/Referred Pain

In the way that the fibrillating heart
diesels out of rhythm, second floor left,

first floor right, and breathtaking pain
skewers the left arm and jaw, or how

the domed dam of the diaphragm, irritated,
sends a hot bolt dissecting diagonally

to the shoulder, pains appearing *here*
may be generated *there*, in a separate quarter

altogether, so that the stab felt so plainly
in your leg must, like love, be attributed

to an upstream short, faulty ground, or
some mysterious disturbance in the field,

snag in the fabric, distorted Memphis
AM station I raised on my new transistor

one summer night, 1967, staticky, tattered:
folks *testifying*, hollering about the *Paraclete*.

It's not that what you feel's not real. *Au
contraire*. It's just rare that the why

you hurt's as plain or pat as the where.

Taking It In to Have It Looked At

In her voice there's Irish tracings,
in her ear a bridgework of bones. In the bones
small sets of shivers upon which
everything you think you hear turns.

In the eye there's carpet receptive
to light waved in from the star; and the tamped
seeds, signaled, splay triggered,
the seeds where the libraries are.

If sleep's dart severs the senses,
then *incommunicado* we drift in our beds; and are
mapped by lovers we never knew
were stowed away strange in our heads.

In Touch

Out back, my mother was hands and knees in the garden,
transported so completely by trowel and transplantation
that the neighbor girl and I had a sure half hour to speed
to the basement, shed clothes, and couple at a speed
incomprehensible to all but nocturnal, burrowing rodents.
And my mother, on the day that I, years later, finally tilled
my own first plot, phoned and spoke to me eloquently
about the spiraling, belled cornucopia, the exotic smells,
the endlessly pleasurable, hand-sampled textures: fine,
sliding carrot seed, milk-spined thistle, the heft of fruit
snapped sweet from the stem. Later, on her one trip

to Boston, we had tea at a Greek café, where two men
sat smoking on a bench near the door, cigarettes in one
hand, rings of worn beads being worried in the other.
I wanted to tell her how right physical therapy seemed
to me: the precise mechanics, the twisting histories,
the privileged questions, positioned limbs, the pivotal
placement of a hand. But she looked, lighting her day's
tenth Kent, so papery and shrunken that we talked
instead about her will, her constant doctoring, the slow
floating she felt, unmoored from the face of the earth.
She would stay in Florida, she'd decided, in the high-rise.
She would find a church. She would get a cat, something
that would pad to her and nose insistently, demanding,
at inexplicable intervals, to be touched.

2.

Two for Getting Out of Bed

1.
Scaffold shifts, foot feels down, tipped spine, segments sliding,
restacks; the pocketknife knee unclasps, the bone rookery's
reconfigured, and the perpendicular, with undying astonishment,
regained. There's the head's weight and woodenness, its brief
calibrating swim, tentative steps, and the slave-cylinder heart
shifting seamlessly to a deeper, more powerful stroke.

You've been away. There's a sense of arrival, a sense of
never having left, a few sidelit objects standing upright
near the door, like things the airlines might've recovered and
brought out last night, separately, with scripted apologies and
signed receipts, by taxi. There ought to be time for a thorough
accounting, but the new day's already dilating, the shower,
shaving, and sock-sort; the rote, inertial slide into the cattle-chute
of another working day. Breathe, run water, raise blinds, bend;
you could do them in your sleep. You are doing them in your
   sleep.

2.
Think of your dreams as sewing done
in Thailand, as a problem you don't completely
understand solved competently, economically,
by skilled workers paid piecework somewhere else. Think
of the tendons in your fingers sliding by

                                                               one another,
of the patterned contractions and tight-cinched rigging
that allows a cupped hand to slip into and lift a small
shimmering lake to your face. Don't think of water and
its daily division from sky, or how it might, in its twisting
and braiding,

                        resemble the soul. Remember
the Jesuits, bent on humiliation, positing the soul to you
as a small wooden chicken. Do not pause, then,
to study yourself naked in the mirror. It profits you,
inevitably, not. Skip,

                             instead, directly to the shower
and let the hissing and spitting needle and rake; let
your skin absorb its beating and pink. The Day is Here
and The Day is Sensational is the cry going up
across the land motherFUCKER! you sing. And why
not? You've been given another chance. And how
many more of those are you scheduled to get?

Copenhagen

Mornings, wakening, I fly back, circle
my body, slip in on an inhalation,
and instantly the electrified muscles
understand everywhere I've been. I
rise and walk, bend my neck, let hot
water lash the length of my back.

I was dreaming about Copenhagen,
about the park near the Tivoli where
clusters of laughing office workers
sunned topless and lunched, while
I stood motionless between trees,
sweating. Last week I thought again

about dying, standing in the kitchen
when our power, unprovoked, tripped
off. I set my knife down on its side
as a deeper silence overtook the day,
then began, slowly, to discriminate leaf
rustle, birdnotes, jets, the faint padding

of the cats' feet on the linoleum,
the usually indifferent cats who, when
agitated, mew and rub their snouts
with increasing urgency against your
body, and, after some days, if the songs
about death are true, reluctantly eat you.

Exsanguination

Think Bleeding Out. Think
aortic aneurysm dissecting down
as you eye the pears in Produce.
Think uprushing floor and
audible, tinder-stick fractures.
Probably dead before he even hit
the deck, the pronouncing doc,
in presumed consolation, offers.
Think of rubber tubing tightened
around your biceps, and the vein
the phlebotomist traces, preps,
pricks; the pint siphoned as you
repose, feet up, reading Chekhov.
Or the G.I. who picked you up in
1975 outside of Twentynine Palms,
then climbed in back, unzipped
his works, tied off and nodded
out as you drove for Vegas, one
crimson pearl in a slo-mo sled
down his arm. Think gut shot

buck, bike-wreck hemophiliac,
lacerated liver, placental abruption,
chainsaw mishap in a mud-slick
woods. Think of the opened
vessel, the closed circuit breached,
the euphemistic gesture of our
impeccably made-up downstairs
neighbor, one arm liquefying
in the white kitchen sink, the other,
weakening, dragging closer, by
its long cord tail, the black,
blocky touchtone phone.

The Dwindles

For weeks, she's eaten little, spoken
less, looking at last like a broom
laid back in a broom closet after
the movers have finished their work.
The bereaved arrive, take her hands,
study her face, swan together with
her labored breathing, which is like
a dull handsaw inching imperceptibly
through a hardwood burl. She exhales,
and it's a long, brow-beating time
before she obliges them with another

inspiration. It's not the long-fenced
soul pushing forward now, but bones,
hieroglyphic, glimmering sensible:
the linked levers of the laid-out limbs,
the skull the secret that's underlined
her face forever. Her skin's slack
parchment, hands and arms wholly
stained with lapped-purple needlestick
bruises. There are the skewed, yellow
toenails, a tangle of IV's and O2,
exhaustion far beyond what the robust

can fathom. There are, by the end,
only her most steadfast attendants:
daughters-in-law, decamped cousins,
knitters. There are stories swapped
in whispers, reminiscences, low hoots
of laughter which she, without opening
her eyes or shifting an inch, as if she
weren't working furiously in some
solitary, unreachable place, smiles at.

On the Surgical Maxim
All Bleeding Eventually Stops

A single spasm sparked roughly
once a second boots the blood in its ten
thousand ramifying, rootbound loops
from the capitol to the distant provinces

and back. You can hear it right now,
knocking like the landlord, throbbing
like the Brookpark Stamping Plant, mid-
graveyard. Its song starts, stops, hard,

hard to imagine, a short of some kind,
a blackening, a breath-taking, a stillness
in which the trailing syncopations
echo a second in your head, and faint

woodwind charts, in minor sixths, merge
with the voices of those *in extremis* being,
on one side, delivered, and on the other,
your lot, decrying their time to depart.

Intact Sensorium

1.
The ear's smithing hammer,
the nap of buds on the tongue,
the spherical eye, tense in its
traces, tracking right, right,
lighting cocked, shot back

to the head of the next line.
The fingertip's discriminations,
gravity's tug on the bones,
the salt tang of the tidelands
in your throat at ebb, so much

information incoming, but you're
thinking about the microbus
of Germans you once watched
undress on the beach below
Viareggio, the Mediterranean

sapphire, the sun a stiletto,
their nude bodies so graceful
and unselfconscious that
you felt a physical longing,
an actual ache in your chest,

a cool hand on your forehead,
an insistent voice saying *Hey,*
you were dreaming, which *no,*
can't be, though you can hear
rain's concussions, the clock's

hum, the two-note accordion
drone of your own breathing,
the relentless drum of someone
pacing agitated, circling the small
kitchen just below you, caged.

2.
A cool drop spirals down
the upturned horn of my ear,
drowns the drum in a calm,
cupped lake. Here's the price

of an ache: music muffled, and
the sound of the poem, in shuffled
snippets, disordered, dotting
the floor. Here's a prayer

that the thing comes together,
like the swarm of redwings
you watched lift, one fluid body,
from a field, or a small engine

reassembling itself from strewn
and scavenged parts, then
throttling up, as if ready, after
brief throatclearing, to speak.

The Bones of the Ear

Where the ear's funneled siphon
tapers down to stem, three bones,
the body's smallest, join drum

to oval window, crucial link,
a sidebent, jewelsmithed bridge
shivering sympathetically with
each captured note of the day's
dense score: faint cock-crows,
rain's run in the gutters, your
own name spoken, bright strand,

middle distance. One Sunday,
in the ICU, I heard a moan so
harrowed, so operatic and other-
worldly, I knew it must've
been someone's last. And from
the hallway, I spied a raisinlike
woman, whitehaired, mouth open,

asleep, and a graying daughter
in a chair alongside, calmly
knitting. I've held, in one cold
lab or another, every bone in
the human skeleton except these.
I've shouted patients' names
an inch from their faces, calling
them back from the fibrillating

edge, teared up at ceremonial
scatterings of ashes, recited
my lines to an empty room to
compare that sound to the one
I'd been hearing, for months
previous, exclusively in my head.

The Muscles of the Face

The front of the skull's alive
with them, dabs, brushstrokes,
dashes, slants, a knifed-on map
of confederated dutchies, a quilt,
a weave, an underlayment of moving
parts, muscles whose single task is
shaping the complex weather playing
over the eloquent plain of the face.

The morphing mask is, in the end,
simple mechanics, solid electrical
engineering: motors and anchors,
feedback loops and force-couples
which embroider, enlarge or eclipse
what's spoken, or to signal, sell
or frankly sabotage in the absence of
actual speech. And working always,
arguably, in the service of a thornier,
more complicated truth. Think

of your mother, young, her face
a sweet treasure reopened exclusively
for you each morning: its comfort,
complexion, dimensions and depth;
its hidden rooms, shadows, silences.
It was the book you learned to read

long before a first *word*, jacketed,
jigsawn, coded, cruel, whirred suddenly
on the page and, with transfiguring, still-
compounding consequences, opened.

Sentinel Falls

presage the downstream series of like, limb-
splintering falls to come, in the unattended
tub, the threshold of Thriftway, the dimly lit,
suddenly syncopating bedroom. Floors and

diagnostics beckon; your vestibular competence
is called into question: bruises bloom, bones
brittle, legs leaden, and you go down hard
with the most trivial perturbations, like some

skillfully dynamited downtown building.
Your well-intentioned children, as you stir
in recovery, determine to sell the house. Now
they see that that first fall was a semaphore,

a signal, a clanging, collaring cowbell. You hit
the ground like some door-pounding prodigal,
announcing, with each shivering concussion,
your unequivocal demand to be readmitted.

Not Turning Away

The God who, earlier this morning, directed
your gaze to the curled, copper, green-veined
madrona leaf resting on the stiff white tips
of the frosted sideyard grass is the same One
who brings you, first patient of the day, the blue
diabetic foot, deep weeping sinus tract and
the unearthly stench that rises from it unshod;

the God who dealt you the science-class hands
and fascination with anaerobes, who guided you,
tripping and thirsty, to the well on the outskirts
of Ashland, where you stared down, saucer-eyed,
at the roped bucket bobbing at the bottom of
the shaft, very like the bucket you'll fetch now
to wash the foot and repack the wound, even
though it's all but certain, from its creeping,

inky edging, that the foot will fall, in a matter
of days, into another bailed bucket, sawn off
mid-shin by a gowned and goggled surgeon with
a reciprocating saw, the God with the leg One
with the God with the saw, who probes the cut
bone of His anaesthetized reflection with a small
steel pick, to determine if the bonestock, at that
point, is viable, or if he'll have to move up a bit
higher, re-cinch the goggles, and cut again.

Joint Play Testing

1.
The hip's capsule's tested
by passively pistoning
the knob of the femur in
the cylinder of the socket,

and the shoulder by
translating the humeral head
east-west forcefully,
suddenly and unannounced.

The kneecap's skate on
the face of the femur,
the mandible's grind
against the maxilla's molars,

the subtle gapping of atlas
on axis when traction's
applied to the skull;
the scapula's tensioned

float on the washboard
of the ribs, the rib-heads
sprung at their ties
to the spine; or the carpals'

shift, like safe tumblers,
as wrist and rays are
extended fully, palm out, in
the universal sign for stop.

2.
Joints, sprung, speak, and
what's said's only appreciated
by hand. We shift or shear
the opposed bones in each
plane of the articulation, and
the rebound's telling; what
we feel we assign words to.

It's a learned skill, like shoe-
tying or slack-wire walking;
the stemmed and radiant gifts
of the world, astonishing,
apprehended first by touch,
taste, eye and ear inform then,
in their turn, those memorably
vivid and affecting others

conjured miraculously from
nothing but these pagebound,
flat-looking fields of words.

Pre-Op Hip

I saw, glancing,
the lights in her eyes:
the tall, narrow windows
of the gym's east wall
curved, bleached,
doubled and creased as
I watched, by a kiting,
lake-blown crow, and
through them

could see the new life
she was struggling to
grasp, where her old,
brittle, fall-fractured
hip was removed while
she slept by a gowned,
gloved, goggled
surgeon, brilliant theater,
reciprocating saw,
and a stainless, nesting
sphere and socket
hammered in, to tightly
engineered tolerances,
in its place. And her

subsequent risings
to standing and thwart-
dodging walks safer,
and, astonishingly,
again unconstrained.
She saw that I saw, said
Will there be pain?
And I said Yes. But less.

Putting Patients in Gowns

What's hidden, we believe,
has something to say. So
we knock, file back, and
part veils to illuminate
a humid place evidently
few have ever seen. There's
a face for it: stoic, blank,
repulsion unregistered,
surprise suppressed, awe
and wonder fastidiously
abjured. For patients, then,
a frank exchange of intimacy
for information, a closer
look conducted with
appropriate permits and
a businesslike bearing.
You arrive at a churchyard;
a pocked, scoured headstone
your new love has driven you,
at twilight, in strained and
uncharacteristic silence, to see.

The Diagnosis of Noisy Knees

Rifle shots, ripping cloth, wood rasps, redacts,
shook rattles, raked gravel, rimshots, maracas, bare-
wire shorts, phone static, dactyls, air brakes, scattered
applause; pistol range, sawblade chatter, gear grit
downshifting, bad front bearing on a hard right turn.
Spilled sugar, half-shell of shot, stage-whisper, slag-
pail, stalk of celery snapped in half every time I

stand. Short string of lacquered firecrackers, crushed
Rice Krispies, valve clatter, roach skitter, trap set,
woodsplitter, ground glass, sharp gasp, birch bark,
stripped; pulp, bank-job tumbler click; syncopated
knock of loose dentures punctuating the What might
it be? she asks wonderingly, thrusting her varicose,
roll-stockinged knee, grapefruit-sized, peppercorn
grinder, out to me.

Exposition

In the slow-drifted, dialing-down day, when
swallows, in legion, crowd onto the high
tension lines above Rt. 10 and kibitz, buzzed
like machinists at the Pearl payday afternoons
singing out in their blue union shopcoats,

I'm listening to my scripture-citing neighbor
Ray tell me the story of the all-midget porn
flick he watched last weekend at an epic
three-day bachelor party that ended in a Portland
suburb with a County Sheriff lightshow and

cruiser convocation, and a dog who looked
like Edward G. Robinson ralphing chunks
of Chinese carryout onto his shoes at 3 a.m.
It's an embroidered story, very like the ones
the new quads and paras try out on staff

a month into rehab, when their girlfriends
have bailed and they slyly produce photos
of their pretzel-bent cars at the wreckers. In
that moment, they say, everything flies past
slo-mo: gravel, stopsign, the pinwheeling, tree-

barking 360, and the consequent transected
cord. Once it was all about dayjobs, backrent,
boss bitches, the chronically-wasted paycheck
to paycheck scuffle. Now, chairbound,
circumspect, they reappraise. It wasn't so

bad, they say. In fact, it was fucking, all
told, great. They want to go back to that last
pint and pipeful, that pivotal, slipped-traction
moment. That flown life; that hard, bitter
thing they hated; *that*. They want that back.

3.

After the Equinox

Now only the transited middle of the day's warm,
the light, in its chapters and gaps, more acute,
the shook-off clothes piled, hems fluttering, on the slats

of the dock. Night's ascendant, and the sun,
rattling around in its crown, barely manages a nickel
glint off the sheared, faceted chop. We coil and go,

plane up and look for our strokes, mules yoked
for a pull. We dig deep enough to check panic,
heart and arms, forge and bellows, rhythm ramped

to a burning, held. Cold paints our throats and bellies,
blues fingertips, and, at ten minutes, turns us.
The shore maples blaze, small cuts welling, a long

way off.

Why It Takes Longer
To Make Love When You're 50

Then, when she reached up for the light switch,
every compass point bent round again to her,
a muscular foreign coupe, brake released, doors
held briefly open, a cosmic cataclysm powerful
enough to rejigger planets in its passing. Now

when she reaches, you see the thinned weave
of her shoulder girdle, the vest-button spine,
quick, provisional holds and releases playing
over her back like a weather map of the High
Plains, the raft of the scapula, high-centered

on crested ribs. How beautiful she is is something
you can go whole days without noticing. Then,
amid the bustle and clutter, you see it, see it
like you see a new moon driving at mid-day,
thumbnailed in a slot between buildings, like you

see the two-point standing three steps deep
in timber, that dappled, fluid line gone stockstill,
coiled, all glossblack eye, dilated pupil, measuring
the clearing, watching you watch.

Woodpecker Tongue

When we were brand-new, still spellbound, flat broke, working graveyard,
and fell into bed most mornings to the shrieks of schoolkids cutting
underneath our window, we saw, two days running, a woodpecker pair,
redcrested, huge, flitting tree to tree in a springtime homehunting tour
down the Sound. And unearthed her *Peterson's* to match its plates of
*pileated*s to our birds, learning that they knock,

                                 then listen for movement:
insects, dinner; and getting sidetracked by a page devoted to the topic
of their tongues. Barbed, sinuous, mobile, measuring, uncoiled, 2/3
the length of their bodies, its origin traced backwards out of their throats,
up over the crowns of their skulls, down between the eye-sockets, and
rooted finally, unambiguously, in the bird's right nostril.

                                         That led us
to songbird tongues, and to coarse, black parrot tongues, then eventually
to the teasing and slow-probing sweetness that seemed back then our
one inalienable, inexhaustible right. We slept and drove to work as
young lovers did the world over, according to our books, surreptitiously
sniffing our fingers, raking distractedly, as the car shuddered to a stop,
through the packed, catacombed glove compartment for a mint.

Small Movements

Pot boiled over, we argued, overdue,
disproportionate, screamed, smashed,
and ended up in the backyard watching
an ant labor heroically, with his crumb,
over the tectonic planks of the picnic table,
the two of us spent, and the coming dusk,
in advancing purples, windless, birdless,
stifling, still. I began then to catalogue

the hundred small movements which
sabotage true stillness: surfaced pulses
at the throat and wrists, the elastic rise
of ribs, the eyes' continuous, small-bore
recalibrations, the blinks, the swallows.
I thought of our parents, the growing
list of Parkinsonian tics and tremors
spontaneously generated, erupting now

with dreamlike logic into their highly
flowered, fastidiously manicured world.
I thought of your face, of the thousand
subtle electronic messages posted there
daily, and of the cramped contortions
teeth, tongue, larynx and lips must
execute simultaneously, fluently, to
produce a single meaningful word.

I grazed a finger past your thumb, and,
to my surprise, you opened your hand
and clasped mine in it, but without
looking at me, slackening the cables

of your neck, or the scoured gray granite
of your face, as if movement and
reciprocal movement were merely
the formal opening gambit of a more

complicated life-and-death contest we'd
now irrevocably admitted ruthlessness to.

Remote Sensing

We watched the redtail kite and carve
the vault above the hayfield, wondering
about the small signals grass must send
as foraging fieldmice, nosing thatch, part
stems, wind works the blonde, seedy tops,
and the whole of the hayfield undulating,
cowlicked, frothed like a sea. Once, in Ohio,

I watched a dowser cross a dry beanfield
waiting for his stick, loosely grasped, to bob.
And the hour that her sister, five states away,
went into labor, my wife, with conviction, knew.
That year, we were renting an efficiency from
a North Dakota widow who rocked summer
nights on her unlit porch, and scared us to death
a hundred times, barking from the shadows ten
feet away as we sorted stoned through our keys.
Rain coming, kids, she'd holler; best check
the windows! Better than any TV weatherman;

claimed she could feel it in her bones. And
what about the ones who paint their foreheads,
wrap up in saffron, roll up their eyes and dance
ecstatically, to tambourines, at airports?
Are they like my long-ago Shaker Heights
girlfriend's graymuzzled dog who struggled up
on arthritic hips and tapped grinning to the door
when our girl was still 10 blocks down Euclid,
blasting Kid Leo, peeling off pantyhose, jumping
stoplights, drumming her hands on the dash?

Icon of St George and the Dragon
on a Souvenir Holycard
from a Russian Orthodox Monastery,
Pskov, Western Russia, 1988

The saint, his halo's disc set off against his rippling
crimson cape, has skewered the dragon remotely, from
high in the saddle of his snowy, long-lashed Arab.
And in a banner across the top, a single word: BEPA,
pronounced *vera*; and meaning not truth, surprisingly,

but *faith*. Now, framed, it hangs on the wall above
our breakfast table where the slant of morning sun
will fire the halo's leaf, and where we traditionally
sit to wrestle with the treacheries laid out in ambush
for us along the nettled, mysteriously circuitous path.

Faith, at a minimum, in the sun's penetrating glance,
its cadenced transit, its ability to stun us, to absolve
sin, to turn us again, in our furrowed, circular pacing,
outward. The knight has lanced the serpent through
its throat, and I imagine the fury with which it whips

and writhes, its strength and energy astonishing, its
razor tail lashing. But look how sadly the saint stares
away, awaiting death's mustering, inevitable coup.
I sip coffee daily wondering what those deep sapphire
eyes have lit on. Swaying grass? Birch copse? Birds?

Broken Spoke

By noon, I've charted on
the taut, bluish, cylindrical leg,
the reconstructed wrist with its plantation
of stitches, the pavement-drummed
nerve which does not currently conduct.
I've explored joint lines, listened
for crepitus, coaxed the offending limbs
to bear a bit more weight. And
the patients, allowing touch, gradually
drop their guards, begin to breathe, to speak,
to delve, without prompt, into intimate,
burdensome things: painful bankruptcies,
incarcerated cousins, a telescope trained
on nudist nextdoor neighbors, an ex
having sex in Vegas with an East Indian
patent lawyer and a tank of nitrous oxide,
recent, compromising falls in the bathroom
which have necessitated the calling

of kids. I built my dream house deep
in the woods, on a firred, mud-rutted road,
and shutter it tight each morning now
since it was cleaned out last winter
by the local Mormon meth manufacturers.
When I wake there winter weekends, sun,
in long shafts, slants in sideways like
a phalanx of fluorescent tubes, like holy-
cards of herald angels, wings pressed
back, long trumpets up. And next to me,
on the desk, is the book I fell asleep
reading, alert, always, for the small word

(I presume smallness) which will stun me,
back me up, change me as a goat
is changed by a blow to the head with
a shovel-blade, as thirsty men are changed
by an inadvertent glimpse of a lake.

Fortune Cookie

Your life, in the barely navigable alley between
some *q* and its *u*, or as your remote, satellite
fingertip successfully separates this very page-
edge from the next, will end, and the hoarse
sobs of your loved ones will, as they inevitably

must, cease. You carry this knowledge the way
you carry radio jingles, antibodies, or the gene
for blue eyes; or the way you carry remodeled
scars, nearly invisible, or crumbs of your exes'
photos in your wallet's vinyl, accordion folds.

Note that I'm positing nothing here you don't
already know, yet I imagine your gaze starting
to weaken, to dial out to the horizon, where there's
always movement, some faintly-lit trajectory you
can track, some strobing you can bird-dog more

easily than you can these flickering days, which
no longer leave even the lightest mark on you, and
blur like passing traffic when you've coasted
smoking to the shoulder, or the fencerow birches
when you're refueled, fixed, fed again, flying.

Wake And Dream

for PJK

The soul takes leave of the body,
the crucifixed nuns in catechism contended, the way the light
withdraws from the day, reluctantly, the pancaked
organdy pinks and purples postcard perfect, pastel-saturated,
two small clouds, cottony and high-gliding, a glint
of gold thread in the hems.

Or: the soul takes leave of the body,
as the hollowed, hack-shaven Jesuits claimed, the way the song's
expelled from the man, reluctantly, rapt room resonating, last note
hewn to four bars, six; vibrato wrung out, die-tapped spiral twining
the trellis, the trapped foot, twisting toward judgment, spat free
finally from the mortal, bog-sucked boot.

I stood next to you at your father's sodded slot
of a grave as you tossed your handful of dirt down
on him and strode off into sleet to underline your dramatic sense of
dislocation which you characterized, characteristically, as vast. I prayed
then, over the priest's weak injunctions, that we might make peace
one day, can you imagine? the two of us fogging the potting shed,
the garden raked supine, sycamores in leaf, the bulbs' tongues,
in swordlike multiples,

                    thrust up. The soul takes leave
of the body, you once told me, the way the trout takes leave
of the lake, reluctantly, dancing its Augustinian, not-today-Lord
dance, reeled into clarity, throwing off spirals lathe-like, the wine-red
velvet-lined case of silver I spilled in the street on the last of your last-
gasp, crosstown moves: you, hungover, sunglassed, stonefaced;
the rest of us out on our hands and knees raking back
the broadcast gleams and stabs.

Addendum to My Father's Advance Directives

What is this thing we'll burn
or bury, and from which we'll withhold,
in deference, all heroic measures? Is it
the temple that the yoga-slim girls of
Hanalei starve and polish night and day?
Is it the dovecote of sanctifying grace?
The sedan-chair of the soul? Is it pure
physics; molecules in a weak matrix of
molecules, vibrating, bound, but destined

long-term, for rebroadcast? Whatever
it is will be, we agree, absent you, and I
imagine it pausing, dropping gracefully
earthward, like spent booster-stage fuel
tanks. We'll stand sunglassed, scanning
skyward for some impossible speck, some
snag in the fabric, until our eyes brim,
blink, lose it. So what can we do

but sing? So long, husk, we'll holler;
Where's the sap in our ham-fist, our
foghorn, shoal, harbor-maker? We're
next is what we'll be thinking, though,
shuffling forward toward the grave's
sodded, backhoed brink. And the bees
will work the ditchside blackberries
in July, combing through the froth
of blossoms, the same ones you, utterly
out-of-character, once ordered us out
of the car to sniff, since they were sweet,
you said, and so briefly worth the welts.

Body Optional

Once, before people and
animals became wholly separate
nations, dreaming could take you
down to the river's swirled surface

and across, fish bending off like
welding sparks, shooting stars a foot
below you. If you ate, you weren't
hungry when you woke. If you visited

a lover, she smiled at you later,
surreptitiously, sidelong, at the market.
The young, so hurried, would forget
where they'd left their bodies, and

had to comb the caves and clearings
for days sometimes, calling. It
was possible to drop the scratched,
heavy, sense-dense thing like a

jacket, and put it back on when your
auntie, the widow, needed a ditch dug.
You could hear music from a mile.
You could waft from school and ride,

unnoticed, on the backs of crocodiles.
Then, in exchange for permission
to hunt, we became inseparable
from our bodies, to give game fair

warning, and the old a longer spell
with the children, to show them knots
and letters and teach them the thousand
side-splitting songs about sex.

Startle Reflex

The newborn body's budlike, compact, raveled
at rest, each joint flexed, drawn tightly in, though
a close clap will cause limbs and spine to extend,
eyes to bug in a look of bewilderment so bone-deep
that a trace of it ghosts our alarmed looks forever.

Brush a bare wire and the world sees in you
astonishment, comedy, recoil, receipt of a message
from an unseen hand; it's a reminder that, within
the quotidian, there are visitations, insinuations,
blindsides and asteroids, all, in the end, devoid of

reason or warning. Dudes, let go of making sense.
Here, a cotton-batten-cloud-decked float labors by
with an ecstatic church choir aboard, heads loose,
shouting and stomping. Followed by the clear
ring of your cell, the message that stops your heart.

Three Falls

1.

There is the telescoped moment
when you *know*, spindle tipped
past fixing; when what's going to
happen's revealed, in its garment
of consequence and inevitability a split

second before it actually does.
In Botticelli's luminous *Annunziata*,
Gabriel speaks soothingly to the kneeling
Virgin, her eyes averted, each of his words
falling solidly, like coins in slots, making

real what she already, before she ever
laid eyes on him, knew. One Sunday
I spent an hour in the ICU with a swiftly
dwindling woman, moving limb to limb, down
each chain, slowly ranging her joints. And

in the end, she opened her eyes,
took my hand, and sang Goodbye, old friend,
goodbye!
        The alarm, the sneeze,
the climax: in the midst of striving, the yard
of birds, unprompted, stops, and you,

without so much as looking up, know;
oh. You have time to twist, shoot out an arm,
surrender. Not that the ground's inclined
to mercy.

2. (3 a.m.)

That deep, hardwired part of you terrified

of falling yanks you back curtly, dog-on-
chain, each time you lapse again toward sleep.
And instead of falling, you are subjected to
calm, fugue-like indictments of yourself, and
anxious examination of the flimsy, cluttered, too-
steep ladder of tomorrow. Back when I *could*

sleep, I would leap regularly in dreams out
into space and feel myself, like a cliff diver,
stall, tip head-down, plunge. And at the last
possible moment, earth uprushing, I would
either startle or pull out and soar, skimming
treetops, straining for a ledge or vantage to
light, take my bearings, and launch out again

swanlike into air. My girlfriends all had deep
Freudian explanations, but I avoided talking
to them about it. I was superstitious and didn't
want to fuck the thing up. I said I thought
certain things were simply better left alone,
unanalyzed, unnamed. To which they replied
Like what? Name one.

3.

She's escaped the Orthopods
with a stainless plate and some screws
in her hip, escaped the opportunistic
pneumocystis which colonizes,
classically, the compromised. But
her house is a trash-maze, she can't
master the walker's waltz cadence,
and she's forthright that she will not
entertain exercise voluntarily. So I lift
the length of her, light as kindling,
on our first day, to the floor,
and ask her to show me how
she would, next fall, get herself

back up. And, too weak in the arms
to prop to all-fours, she lies there
charming and tells me about her
sentinel fall, the light she saw
hitting the linoleum: one quick spark,
blue; not death, she understood
immediately, but death's baptist, Pain,
preparing the ground, calling hoarse
through the screendoor with a fist
full of wilted sweet pea. That

shock woke some numb, long-sidelined
part of her, and for that she conjures
gratitude. But he's here now first
thing each morning, birdlegged,
dream-pale, like some shrill, breathtaking
alarm you don't remember setting,
and, can't now, groping blindly and
bolt-upright, figure out how to turn off.

Bodying Up

A square, velvety, scallop-edged black and white
of the Kelly brothers in their St Malachi jerseys,
August, '44, a month after they threw their father
out and his clothes in a suitcase after him, and his
flask as an afterthought at the back of the Packard.

A freelance wolfpack, maybe; the too-pale eyes,
the picketed teeth, lean slouches, alertness. What's
striking is how much they resemble each other, and,
my wife insists, how much they resemble a younger
me; the narrow face and shoulders, she says, the lips.

Mike, the second oldest, down from Alaska in 1969,
bloodied my nose with an elbow in a friendly evening
3 on 3, bodying me up for a rebound. Do that to wake up
the other guy, he suggested, early on in a big game,
when the ref and the action's flown upcourt. Then

he spat, winked and smiled, a gesture identical in
rhythm and timing to one I'd despised in my own father
from time immemorial, and which I now trot out myself
on occasion, according to the resident genetics expert,
without, she's convinced, having any idea I'm doing it.

Unbecoming

One night the bright new therapist everyone
was secretly in love with stacked up her charts,
scattered goodbyes, walked to her car, drove
to New Mexico, cut off her hair and renounced
worldly things, rising each morning at 4 a.m.
to chant in a stony dojo and sit alertly, quietly,
sun kindling, plumes of steam jetting cylindrically,
swirled prayers, from her nose. She wrote us
a card with her new name which meant *Servant
of Creation*. We wrote back on clinic letterhead
Servant, Come home! and signed our names with

flourishes. I saw then that all she had made
herself had not been enough to make her happy,
and that her mission now was to thoroughly
undo it, ripping out stitch after miscounted stitch
until she had shredded her suffocating garment,
and could tramp once more among the lowly
roadside flora, the leggy yarrow, bristling thistle,
grasping morning glory, feeling only awe and
gratitude, seeing the right hand of God at work.

I admired her courage. What great thing was
my life anyway, but some operatic farce of
loud alarms, late charges, and locustlike teens
with joysticks obliterating civilizations joyfully?
Last week I found a possum in the garage
who'd been living for God knows how long
inside the back of the freezer, who hissed as I
skidded the big white chest to the driveway,
and bolted, after some strategic prodding with

a rakehandle, bristly and blackeyed for the woods,
shouting boys in pack pursuit. And I, surprisingly
shaky, scraped the massive freezer back into
the garage and plugged it in, thinking of the stink
and ugliness of the creature, which I know isn't
right, and reviewing the facts, ordering events,
pulling together on some wide, half-conscious
table, the story I knew I'd be telling you, with
embroidery and comic digressions, soon.

Comealong

Ralph, in the rain, wrapped
the maple with a chain and
the corner post with a cable,
and put the comealong, like
a pastor's hand, between them.

And with each ratchet,
the fencerow came, soldier
by soldier, to attention, and
the stapled wires between
posts, for a rising second, sang.

We recollared the corner
in a yard of concrete, and
left it the weekend to cure,
then met again Monday to see
if it would stay up on its own.

Ralph's arms, thinned with
the cancer, swam inside his
billowing sleeves, but his still-
callused hands went confidently
to the comealong, and, by

ratcheted increments,
slackened it. The trued fence,
in mixed morning birdsong,
sang briefly backwards, dropping
octaves, and, as Ralph said

it would, stood.

Wholesale Changes

The falls fell
from the sky-
blue hole high
above the dank
green grotto,
a sunburnt, two-
hour climb from
where we now

stood, stripped,
and wordlessly
waded into chill,
billowing mist,
and stonewalled
roar and roil.
And the steely

column of water
drumming down,
piledriving our
skulls, spintering
silver and so
painfully cold we
both heard bells.